TULIPS

TULIPS

PETER ARNOLD

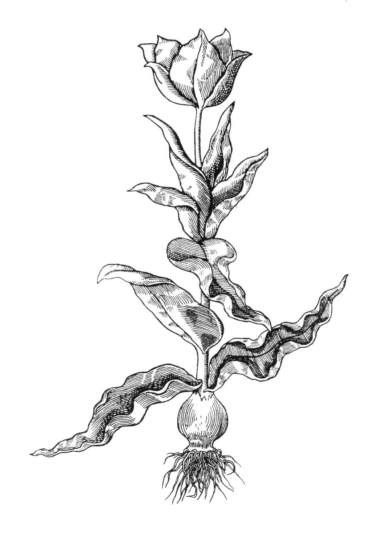

MACMILLAN PUBLISHING COMPANY
NEW YORK

MAXWELL MACMILLAN INTERNATIONAL
NEW YORK   OXFORD   SINGAPORE   SYDNEY

Text and photographs copyright © 1992 by Peter Arnold
Design and typesetting copyright © 1992 by Breslich & Foss

Conceived and produced by
Breslich & Foss
Golden House
28–31 Great Pulteney Street
London W1R 3DD

Designed by Nigel Partridge

Macmillan Publishing Company
866 Third Avenue
New York, NY 10022

Macmillan Publishing Company is part of the Maxwell Communication
Group of Companies.

Library of Congress Cataloging-in-Publication Data

Arnold, Peter, Photographer.
    Tulips / Peter Arnold.
        p.   cm.
    ISBN 0–02–503251–8
    1. Tulips.   2. Tulips—Pictorial works.   I. Title.
SB413.T9A76   1992
635.9′34324—dc20   92–9722
                                                        CIP

Macmillan books are available at special discounts for bulk
purchases for sales promotions, premiums, fund-raising, or
educational use. For details, contact:

Special Sales Director
Macmillan Publishing Company
866 Third Avenue
New York, NY 10022

10 9 8 7 6 5 4 3 2 1

Printed in Italy

Peter Arnold would like to thank James and Wendy Akers, Sybil Arnold, Walter Bloms,
Vivien Bowler, Andy Boyton, Paula Breslich, Timothy Clark, Barry Holmes, Judy Martin,
Nigel Partridge, Danny Pope, Stevie Robertson and Loraine at Ilford, Springfields
Gardens, Aaron So and Laura Wilson.

Illustration on page 2 from Chrispijn van de Passe, *Hortus Floridus* (c. 1650), page 3
from Mattioli, *Commentarii* (1565), page 5 from Conrad Gesner, *De Hortis Germaniae*
(1561), pages 6, 7, 8, 9, 10, 11 from Basilius Besler, *Hortus Eystettensis* (1613).

CONTENTS

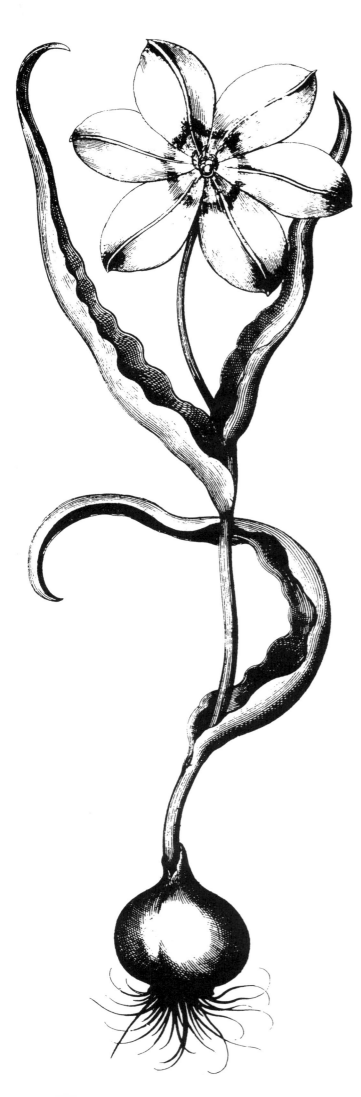

INTRODUCTION

I am a keen gardener, and I have always grown tulips in my garden. The sturdiness of the plants appeals to me as much as the physical beauty of the blooms. When I began to plant my garden, I decided to include tulips because I knew they were easy to grow — you just plant the bulbs, leave them over the winter, and then you are rewarded in the spring with the most glorious display of colours. When the flowers finish, you just dig up the bulbs and dry them out, then store them until you are ready to plant them again the following autumn. Although I knew they would come up year after year, they constantly surprised me with their vivid hues and perfect shapes.

It seemed a natural progression that I should include tulips in my photographic studies: the multitude of colours — some so brilliantly intense and striking, others so delicate — the individual flower shapes and forms, all cried out to be photographed. I began to see tulips with quite a different eye. I felt compelled to investigate further the secret of the tulip, and what it was that created these marvellous "freaks."

After the bleakness of winter, tulips offer a symbol of regrowth and recovery, and this was the underlying inspiration for my decision to celebrate the tulip through my work as a photographer. The project was given impetus on a visit to my sister in the United States. I had sent her some tulip bulbs the previous year, and arrived to find the gardens around her home on fire with vibrant Dutch colour. This was the spur I needed, and I started work immediately I returned to England.

When I began collecting suitable specimens for my photographic studies, I was disappointed by the limited range of tulips that was readily available. In England, the market is mainly geared to a few best-selling, long-lasting varieties that are particularly suitable as cut flowers. I toured the country, following up information on places where unusual or interesting varieties of tulips were grown, and I also made several trips to Holland. The tulips I brought back were kept under a tunnel of plastic sheeting specially constructed to protect the flowers from the weather and bugs, whilst allowing them to open in full light.

I wanted my photographs to show both the astonishing range of tulip types and the splendour of the individual blooms, so I decided to work in the studio, using my experience in fashion and beauty photography to compose detailed, close-up studies. To focus attention on the forms, colours and textures of the flowers, I posed them against black or white backgrounds only. I used a Hasselblad camera and an electronic flash unit, with either a single light source or an extra flash head on the background to create greys.

It was difficult to photograph so many flowers of the same genus and obtain enough variation to maintain interest. Each shot had to be carefully composed to bring out the representational characteristics of the individual flower. Such concentrated work was quite a test of my own enthusiasm, but the more I became involved with the "tulip portraits," the more my interest in these beautiful flowers increased. I also researched the history of the tulip and learned details of its cultivation, and gradually acquired a library of specialist writings.

Although the tulip was a late addition to garden culture in the West, its impact was immediate and lasting. It is unique among flowers for having been the subject of extraordinary financial speculation — the "tulipmania" that erupted in seventeenth-century Holland, resulting in vast fortunes being made and lost in the trade of tulip bulbs. Tulips are also big business in modern times. Although most people primarily associate Holland with tulip production, the bulb industry in Japan is now much larger than that in Holland. There are also important growing areas in Britain, France — especially the south — and the United States. It is an unsentimental business; the beautiful flower heads are all cut off in their prime so that the goodness in the plant is not wasted on reproduction, but retained to promote development of the new bulbs. However, the use of these flower heads has resulted in spectacular displays at the annual tulip festivals.

Since tulips were first cultivated in the West almost four centuries ago, the decorative qualities of their elegant blooms have been celebrated by artists and craftsmen in many countries. The tulip appears in paintings, prints and manuscripts, on ceramics and fabrics, in metalwork and engravings, and in architectural ornament. In my collection of seventeenth-century botanical prints, some of the most beautiful images are of tulip flowers. I also collect seventeenth-century Chinese porcelain; many pieces were sent to Holland and England at the time of tulipmania, and the blue-and-white decoration sometimes includes tulip motifs.

Today, there are more than three thousand named varieties of tulip. Although my photographs show only a small range, I hope I have succeeded in capturing their intriguing qualities and that readers will be inspired to share my enthusiasm for these unique flowers.

THE ORIGIN OF THE GARDEN TULIP

It is often assumed that the tulip is native to Holland, since its major role in Dutch history and importance to Holland's modern-day economy are well known. However, the natural distribution of the tulip — or genus *Tulipa*, as it is correctly named — ranges from the mountainous foothills on both sides of the Mediterranean through Asia Minor and Central Asia, and includes Iran, Afghanistan, northern India and China.

The first documented reference to the tulip by a European dates from 1554, in a letter written by Ogier Ghiselin de Busbecq, Viennese ambassador to the Ottoman court of Sultan Suleiman the Magnificent. Busbecq described how, when travelling from Adrianople to Constantinople in Turkey, "An abundance of flowers was everywhere offered to us — Narcissus, Hyacinths, and those which the Turks call 'Tulipam', much to our wonderment, because of the time of the year, it being almost the middle of winter, so unfriendly to flowers." He also noted the lack of fragrance in these otherwise perfect "Tulipam" flowers. Even today, it is commonly thought that tulips have no scent. However, my research has revealed a few varieties which are scented, nearly all with orange or yellow-orange colouration; *Tulipa* 'Orange Favourite' on page 30 is one of them.

The tulip had been held in high esteem for a long time in the Middle East, and was adopted as an emblem of the Turkish court. The Turks had been cultivating tulips at least since the beginning of the sixteenth century and had taken great trouble to develop new and interesting varieties; beautiful specimens were enthusiastically bought and sold. The Turks preferred the "lyre"-shaped flower with its long pointed petals, a form closely related to that of the species flower and similar to today's "lily-flowered"' tulips.

It appears that Busbecq misinterpreted the name given to the flower, and this error has been perpetuated throughout its history. The Persian name *lale* is the Turkish word for tulip. The genus name is derived from the Persian words *thoulyban* or *tulipant*, or the Turkish word *tulband*, all meaning "turban." Busbecq probably misunderstood an interpreter who was comparing the shape of the flower to a turban.

Busbecq sent tulips from Turkey to Emperor Ferdinand I of Germany, and brought back seeds on his return. Possibly he also imported some bulbs; tulips take up to seven years to flower from seed, but it is documented that within five years of his return tulip flowers were to be seen in the gardens of Austria. This may imply that Busbecq's tulips were not in fact the first to be imported. Although

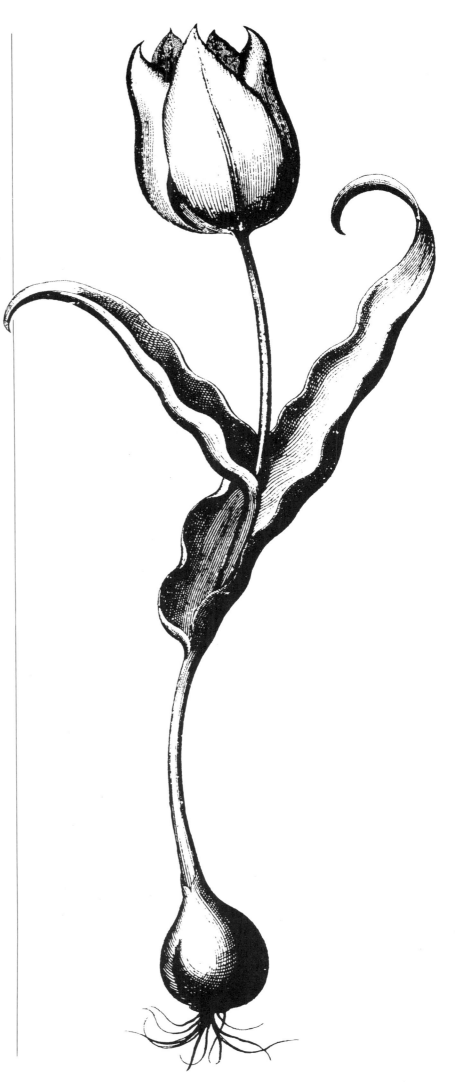

sources disagree as to the exact date of the introduction of the tulip to Europe, its presence was confirmed in April 1559 by the German naturalist Conrad Gesner, who recorded seeing "a single large reddish flower like a red lily" in the garden of Councillor John Henry Herwart at Augsburg.

These first tulips were named after Gesner — *Tulipa gesneriana*, a bright red flower with a dark base. Many of the present-day cultivated forms have been derived from this plant by cross-breeding it with other botanical or wild species, and also with new cultivars.

Throughout sixteenth-century Europe, there was increasing interest in new plants and garden cultivation. The first mention of tulips in the early herbal books appeared in Dodeon's *De Stirpium Historia* (1553) and the first illustrations were printed in Conrad Gesner's *De Hortis Germaniae Liber* (1561) and Mattioli's *Historia Plantarum* (1561).

THE TULIP IN HOLLAND

Some of the plants brought back to Europe by Busbecq were procured by the renowned horticultural expert Carolus Clusius, then prefect to the Royal Medicinal Garden in Prague. Forced by a religious dispute to leave his home and resettle in Holland, he was subsequently appointed Professor of Botany at Leiden, the university city on the Dutch coast, where he became curator of the Hortus Botanical Gardens, which still exist today and are open to the public. Here Clusius experimented with tulip cultivation and was responsible for popularizing these unfamiliar, gloriously coloured flowers. This was the beginning of Holland's special association with tulip culture.

Because tulips were so well suited to formal garden displays, they rapidly gained popularity among the wealthy and fashionable classes and soon graced the gardens of Austria, Germany, Flanders and the Lowlands. Enthusiasts were inspired to experiment with cross-breeding, and many new and different varieties were produced. Demand forced prices up, and this soon created financial speculation, initially in France but spreading rapidly northwards through Flanders to Holland, which then saw the most astonishing drama in the history of horticulture – the phenomenon known as tulipmania or "The Wind Trade."

TULIPMANIA

This extraordinary turn of events in Dutch history is well documented, and evolved from a particular characteristic of the tulip plant. Unlike other plants, which can vary their form only by natural mutation and cross-breeding, tulips have an unpredictable tendency to "break" or "rectify," thereby changing their appearance. A bulb whose flower is true-coloured to variety can unexpectedly change and create a "broken" bloom with new and unusual colouration or form. Generally, the flowers may become variegated with colourful stripes or blotches, or they may disfigure to create a new and distinctive petal shape. Once the plant has "broken," the flower remains variegated, and propagation from offset bulbs reproduces the changed form of the mother plant. It is a characteristic that can occur even after the tulip has been true-coloured for several years. *Tulipa* 'Burgundy Lace' is photographed here in its true-coloured form (page 21), in a "broken" form (page 20) and as a natural mutation or "sport" (page 80). It is now known that this "breaking" characteristic is caused by a viral infection, but in the early days of tulip cultivation it seemed to be a spontaneous phenomenon — it was this perplexing trait that captured the imaginations of the early admirers. Since horticulturists did not know why the changes occurred, it became a challenge to experiment with cross-breeding in the hope of producing even more exquisite and unusual variants.

Trading in tulip bulbs on a large scale had begun as early as 1623, but tulipmania was at its height between 1634 and 1636. These strange and novel tulip forms were much sought after, and they became a status symbol, a luxury that only the very rich could afford. Broken tulips similar to those now classified as Rembrandts were the most desirable, and the inflated value of the most unusual blooms was epitomized by a flower called "Semper Augustus," red and white with a blue-tinted base, which sold for thousands of florins. *Tulipa* 'Zomershoon' (page 53) was also a favourite of the period, and dates from 1620.

Enthusiastic amateur growers all had high hopes of cultivating a prize bloom that would make them rich overnight. A frenzied atmosphere developed, and tulip societies were set up in the taverns of most towns to discuss the merits of certain rare blooms and to organize the buying and selling of bulbs. At first, sales took place only after the bulbs had flowered and the quality of the flowers had been judged. However, as greedy speculation increased, sales took place all year round, even when the bulbs were still below ground. It was a sheer gamble to predict what the bloom would look like, and this made any dealing liable to abuse and fraud.

As dealing gathered momentum, tulips changed hands for completely unrealistic prices. There are records of a house being sold for three tulip bulbs. To stay in the market, people started to mortgage their houses and, in some cases, whole estates were sold to cover the cost of tulip bulbs. Craftsmen even sold the essential tools of their trade in order to buy bulbs. This speculation became ludicrous but as there was such a tremendous market for tulips for a while, everyone made a profit. More often than not, the bulbs were never handed over — possibly they did not even exist. In summer, when it was the customary time to make settlement, the dealer often either received the difference by which the bulbs had increased in value or paid out the amount by which the value had depreciated.

Inevitably this artificial market became saturated, and late in 1636 it suddenly crashed. Dealing ceased with everyone wanting to sell bulbs and no one offering to buy. The situation developed into a catastrophe on a national scale and in February 1637, delegates from the principal towns of Holland gathered in Amsterdam to try to resolve the situation. It was agreed that all tulip sales made before a certain date should be binding; and transactions made after that date could be cancelled if notice was given within an agreed period. Unfortunately this did not work in practice, and so many lawsuits were filed with the courts that the legal system came to a complete standstill.

In April 1637 the Court of Holland declared that any vendor who could not make his purchaser pay up could dispose of the bulbs himself and claim the difference by which the selling price fell short of the original contract. Many sellers were unable to obtain what was due to them and eventually cut their losses, accepting cash settlements sometimes representing as little as five percent of what they were owed. Many more did not get paid at all. Thousands were bankrupted and their lives ruined. Tulipmania came to an abrupt end.

THE TULIP IN ENGLAND

It seems that tulips arrived in England in 1577 or 1578. This date can only be roughly calculated from a few documented references, including one in John Gerarde's famous herbal, published in 1597. It is clear that tulip growing was well-established in England by the early seventeenth century. John Parkinson, author of the influential gardening book *Paradisi in Sole* (1629), captured their aesthetic appeal in his exquisite flower engravings, and in the text described 140 varieties of tulip that were common in English gardens at the time, including *Tulipa* "The Turkes Cap". Tulips received the royal seal of approval through John Tradescant, gardener to King Charles I, who cultivated fifty different varieties in the royal gardens. In 1636, the year before tulipmania ended in Holland, tulips were offered — unsuccessfully — as a commodity on the London Exchange. They continued to be great favourites in the gardens of the aristocracy until the middle of the eighteenth century.

Unfortunately, as more tulip varieties became available, their novelty receded and they lost their fashionable status in formal gardens. But among horticulturists of the eighteenth and nineteenth centuries, there was a continuing effort to improve stock and create the perfect tulip. The Dutch had already produced a "florist's tulip," with shorter, broader petals than the species flowers, and this was used as the basis for tulip breeding by English growers. Experimentation resulted in a flower with

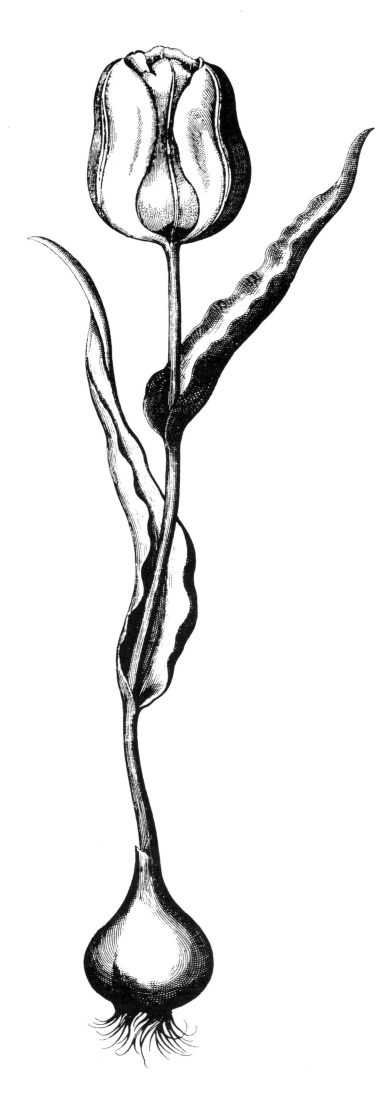

short, rounded petals, the shape of the bloom almost hemispherical and likened to that of a claret glass. Tulips were bred to secure this shape and to develop regular patterns in petal markings. The first definition in English of a florist's tulip was in Miller's *Gardener's Dictionary* of 1731, and this became the basis for standards of old-English tulips, today called English florist's tulips.

By 1820, the English florist's tulip had become highly refined and the flower had been developed to an open cup shape, with a clear, unstained base, to show off the inside markings to better effect (for example, *Tulipa* 'James Wild' on page 79). At first the main growers were concentrated in the affluent south, but around 1640 new seedlings were produced in the north, and tulips became affordable to the common man. The nineteenth century produced many keen gardeners and amateur tulip enthusiasts. Tulip societies were set up to organize exhibitions of the flowers, and The National Tulip Society was formed in 1849 to regulate standards. Interest reached its height in the 1850s. More recently, florist's tulips have gone into decline, but the fine tradition of their cultivation has been continued by the Wakefield and North of England Tulip Society and enthusiasm for these tulips is growing once again.

Garden tulips originally derived from Dutch stock became equally popular, but they were considered to be decorative additions to the garden rather than competition flowers. In general, they were either bred haphazardly or occurred as a result of natural cross-breeding, and they had no consistent form or habit. Little recorded data existed on breeding patterns of these tulips, and there were no guidelines for their classification. A group of keen growers decided to rectify the situation and systematically searched for fine specimens, which they recorded and collectively named cottage tulips. In the early twentieth century, this group was reclassified and divided into three separate categories — Darwin tulips, English tulips and Dutch tulips. Enthusiasm for Darwin tulips encouraged a movement towards commercialized growing in England.

Many Dutch bulb sellers had come to England, and some settled and established themselves as tulip growers. It was due to their expertise that Lincolnshire became the centre of the English bulb industry towards the end of the nineteenth century. Fenland was drained and converted to growing fields. In particular, the silty soil around the town of Spalding proved to be similar to that in parts of Holland, and ideal for tulip cultivation. By the 1920s, flower production was in full force and has continued to thrive.

THE TULIP IN NORTH AMERICA

Tulips have been grown in America from the earliest days of colonial settlement. Some bulbs and seed were taken by European emigrants in their luggage along with other personal possessions; others were sent for by the settlers once they had established themselves in their new country. Tulip flowers are a common motif in paintings and domestic decoration — on items ranging from dishes to quilts — dating from the eighteenth century. Documentary evidence includes the planting lists and gardening notes of Thomas Jefferson, who grew beds of tulips and hyacinths for spring colour on his estate at Monticello.

The ready availability of tulips in nineteenth-century America is suggested by a press advertisement for a nursery in Boston, Massachusetts, published in 1860, listing fifty different varieties of tulip among its stock. Perhaps more significant was the establishment in Michigan of a colony of Dutch settlers during the first half of the nineteenth century. This became the town of Holland, now the site of one of the United States' major tulip festivals.

The United States has some important growing areas supplying its domestic bulb trade, although bulbs are also imported in large quantities directly from Holland. As in European countries, there have been fashions and preferences for particular tulip varieties: American gardeners often favour single-coloured flowers, whereas in Europe blooms with dramatically marked petals are more popular. In the United States a number of formal gardens maintain ornamental tulip beds, in keeping with the original flower-bed plans when the gardens were first laid out in the eighteenth and nineteenth centuries.

Possibly the largest public display of tulips in North America — including as many as 200 different varieties — is in the Canadian capital city of Ottawa, where an annual spring festival has been held since 1951. Canada has a special affinity for tulips, partly because of its ties with the Dutch Royal Family. During World War II, Canada gave refuge and hospitality to Queen Juliana of the Netherlands and her family. In gratitude for this and for the help of the Canadian Armed Forces in the liberation of Holland, she sent the people of Canada a gift of 100,000 tulip bulbs. This gift has been continued by Queen Beatrix and the Dutch people in subsequent years. Today, extensive tulip displays can also be seen in Vancouver, Montreal and Toronto.

TODAY'S TULIP INDUSTRY

Bulb growing is now an important worldwide industry incorporating modern scientific technology and control. Tulips are traded throughout the world as both cut flowers and bulbs, with all new varieties being recorded in the Classified List and International Register of Tulip Names by the Royal General Bulbgrowers' Association of Holland.

The traditional bulb field sites are still mainly concentrated between the cities of Haarlem and Leiden — the heart of the industry. The sandy soil of the flatlands behind the Dutch coastal dunes is ideal for tulips, and although this is no longer the largest bulb-growing area of the world, it has the most historic associations. The Hortus Bulborum Garden at Limmen in the district of Noord has established a comprehensive collection of older varieties of tulip. In 1928, it was noticed that many old species were dying out and it was decided that a determined effort should be made by the Garden to perpetuate bulb cultivars of historical importance and varieties that were in danger of disappearing or had gone out of production, as well as all the new registered varieties. More recently, a museum has been opened at Lisse dedicated to the Dutch bulb industry.

As in Holland, the main English growing sites have proved to be major tourist attractions. Since 1959, Spalding has held an annual flower parade, with colourful floats richly decorated with brilliantly coloured tulip heads. There is also Springfields in Spalding, a permanent garden site linked to the growing fields, where in April and May each year there is a spectacular display of tulips covering some twenty acres.

The tulip was not introduced into Japan until trading links with other countries opened up at the end of the nineteenth century. The first bulbs were imported by Dutch merchants and the industry began to develop during the 1920s. Japan now produces 120 million spring bulbs each year; many growers combine tulip cultivation with a main crop of rice. The primary areas of production are Toyama and Niigata prefectures, on Japan's west coast, where the climate is temperate and similar to that of Holland. Both sites host tulip festivals and there are other spring flower festivals in which tulips feature prominently.

In North America there are many spring flower festivals, and formal public plantings usually include displays of tulips. A drive through the Skagit Valley in Washington State during early May will reveal acres of tulip fields, a sight not to be bettered anywhere in the United States.

In Australia, there are four important tulip festivals and the main growing areas are based around Silvan-Monbulk in the Dandenong Ranges of Victoria and, more recently, in Tasmania.

Major events and displays of tulips are listed on the following page, together with details of tulip bulb suppliers.

BULB SUPPLIERS

Note: In parts of the world where there is no pronounced cold season, tulip bulbs require a period of cold before planting, and suppliers can provide bulbs which have been cold-treated artificially.

UNITED KINGDOM

Jacques Amand Ltd.
The Nurseries
Clamp Hill, Stanmore
Middx HA7 3JS

Avon Bulbs
Upper Westwood
Bradford-on-Avon
Wilts BA15 2AT

Jacques Bakker Holland
P.O. Box 111, Spalding
Lincs PE12 6EL

Walter Blom & Son Ltd.
Coombelands Nurseries
Leavesden, Watford
Herts WD2 7BH

Rupert Bowlby
Gatton, Reigate
Surrey RH20 0TA

Broadleigh Gardens
Barr House, Bishops Hull
Taunton, Somerset TA4 1AE

Cambridge Bulbs
40 Whittlesford Road
Newton, Cambridge CB2 5PH

P. de Jager & Sons Ltd.
The Nurseries, Marden
Kent TN12 9BP

Gee Tee Bulb Co. Ltd.
Matmore Gate, Spalding
Lincs PE11 2PN

W.E. Ingwersen Ltd.
Birch Farm, Gravetye
Nr. East Grinstead
West Sussex RH19 4LE

Moolinaar Horti Group
Hoffleet Stow, Bicker
Boston, Lincs PE20 3AF

Paradise Centre
Twinstead Road, Lamarsh
Bures, Suffolk CO8 5EX

J. Parker (Dutch Bulbs)
452 Chester Road,
Old Trafford,
Manchester M16 9HL

Potterton & Martin
Cottage Nursery, Moortown Road
Nettleton, Caistor,
Lincs LN7 6HX

O.A. Taylor & Sons Bulbs Ltd.
Washway House Farm
Holbeach, Spalding
Lincs PE12 7PP

Thompson & Morgan
London Road, Ipswich
Suffolk IP2 0BA

Van Tubergen UK Ltd.
Bressingham, Diss
Norfolk IP22 2AB

Wavex Pergola Ltd.
Anchor Road, Terrington St. Clements
Norfolk PE34 4HL

NORTHERN IRELAND

'Knowehead'
15 Ballynahatty Road, Omagh
Co. Tyrone BT78 1PN

AMERICA

Bakker of Holland
U.S. Reservation Center
Louisiana, MO 63353-0050
Tel: (314) 454-4525

Breck's
U.S. Reservation Center
6523 North Galena Road
Peoria, IL 61656
Tel: (309) 691-4616

Brooksfield Farm
426 Byrd Street
Centralia, WA 98531
Tel: (206) 736-8209

Bundles of Bulbs
112 Green Springs Valley Road
Owings Mills, MD 21117
Tel: (301) 363-1371

W. Atlee Burpee and Co.
300 Park Avenue
Warminster, PA 18991-0003
Tel: (212) 674-4900

Peter de Jager Company
188 Asbury Street, P.O. Box 2010
Hamilton, MA 01982
Tel: (508) 468-4707

Dutch Gardens, Inc.
P.O. Box 200
Adelphia, NJ 07710
Tel: (908) 780-2713

Heritage Gardens
1 Meadow Ridge Road
Shenandoah, IA 51601-0700
Tel: (605) 665-5188

Jackson and Perkins
1 Rose Lane
Medford, OR 97501-9811
Tel: (503) 776-2000

Mad River Imports
P.O. Box 269, North Fayston Road
Moretown, VT 05660
Tel: (802) 496-3004

McClure & Zimmerman
P.O. Box 368, 108W Winnebago
Friesland, WI 53935
Tel: (414) 326-4220

Messelaar Bulb Company
P.O. Box 269, Country Road
Route 1A
Ipswich, MA 01938
Tel: (508) 356-3737

Netherlands Bulb Company
2 Cypress Peak Lane
Montvale, NJ 07645
Tel: (201) 573-0363

Quality Dutch Bulbs
P.O. Box 225, 50 Lake Drive
Hillsdale, NJ 07642
Tel: (215) 253-9570

John Scheepers, Inc
RD 6 Phillipsburg Road
Middletown, NY 10940
Tel: (914) 342-1135

Smith and Hawken
25 Corte Madera
Mill Valley, CA 94941
Tel: (415) 383-4415

Thompson & Morgan
P.O. Box 1308
Jackson, NJ 08527
Tel: (908) 363-2225

Van Bourgondien Brothers, Inc.
245 Farmingdale Road, P.O. Box A
Babylon, NY 11702
Tel: (516) 669-3523 or (800) 645-5830

Van Engelen, Inc.
313 Maple Street
Litchfield, CT 06759
Tel: (203) 567-5662

Mary Mattison van Schaik
RR 1 Box 181
Cavendish, VT 05142-9725
Tel: (802) 226-7338

Vandenberg
3 Black Meadow Road
Chester, NY 10918
Tel: (914) 469-2633

Veldheer Tulip Gardens
12755 Quincy Street
Holland, MI 49424
Tel: (616) 399-1900

CANADA

Bagnall's Garden Centre
Riverside Drive
P.O. Box 997
Charlottetown,
Prince Edward Island C1A 7M4
Tel: (902) 566-5301

Civic Garden Centre
777 Lawrence Avenue East
North York, Ontario
M3C 1P2
Tel: (416) 445-1552

Cruickshank's
1015 Mount Pleasant Road
Toronto, Ontario
M4P 2M1
Tel: (416) 488-8292

Eagle Lake Nurseries Ltd.
P.O. Box 819
Strathmore, Alberta
T0J 3H0
Tel: (403) 934-3622

Farquarson Farms
1300 Comox Road
Courtenay, British Columbia
V9N 3P6
Tel: (604) 338-8194

Lakeland Plant World
909 Main Street
Dartmouth, Nova Scotia
B2W 3V2
Tel: (402) 435-1983

MacArthur's Nurseries Registered
232 McLaughlin Drive
Moncton, New Brunswick
E1A 4P7
Tel: (506) 859-8999

Sheridan Nurseries
Dollard Garden Centre
3000 Rue de Marche
Dollard-des-Ormeux, Quebec
H9B 2Y3
Tel: (514) 685-3640

Wascana Greenhouses & Nurseries Ltd.
Highway No. 1 East
P.O. Box 314
Regina, Saskatchewan
S4P 3AI
Tel: (306) 757-9090

AUSTRALIA

Broersen Seeds & Bulbs
365 Monbulk Road
Silvan, Vic 3795

Lake Nurseries
439 Silvan Road
Monbulk, Vic 3793

Tesselaar's Padua Bulb Nurseries
357 Monbulk Road
Silvan, Vic 3705

Van Diemen Quality Bulbs
RSD20, Table Cape
Wynyard, Tas 7325

Windy Hill Flowers
Macclesfield Road
Monbulk, Vic 3793

HOLLAND

Walter Blom & Zn.
Hyacintenlaan 2
2182 DE Hillegom

Frans Roozen B.V.
Vogelnzangseweg 49
2114 BB Vogelenzang

Van Turbergen B.V.
Achterwag 33
2161 DV Lisse

Fa. W.S. Warmenhoven
P.O. Box 221
2180 AE Hillegom

J.B. Wijs & Zn Zaadhandel B.V.
Binnenhof 46
1181 ZH Amstelveen

FESTIVALS

UNITED KINGDOM

Tulip Festival
Spalding, Lincolnshire
Annually in April/May
Features a parade of decorated floats along a four-mile route, and floral displays. Springfields Gardens in Spalding have a display of tulips every spring.

AUSTRALIA

Note: In the Southern hemisphere, the flowering season is in September and October.

Tulip Festival
Silvan, Victoria
Annually from mid-September to mid-October
The Silvan festival is organized by Tesselaar's (address above), whose garden and tulip farm are open to the public.

AMERICA

Tulip Time
Holland, Michigan
Annually in May
Special plantings of tulips in streets and parks; exhibits relating to the Dutch settlers of Holland, Michigan; parades and concerts.

Tulip Festival
Orange City, Iowa
Annually in May
Tulip plantings; flower show; parade; street events, music and dancing.

Tulip Time
Pella, Iowa
Annually in May
Tulip plantings and parades.

CANADA

Festival of Spring
Ottawa
Annually in May
Tulip plantings and floral displays.

Both the Royal Botanical Gardens, Hamilton and the Botanical Gardens, Montreal have tulip displays in spring.

HOLLAND

Tulip Festival
Keukenhof Gardens, Lisse
Annually in April/May
Parade of decorative floats organized by the Keukenhof Gardens, who have a tulip display in spring.

Tulip Festival
Bloemen Corso, Lisse
Annually in April/May
Parade of decorated floats and displays.

Floriade
Every 10 years (most recently, 1992)
Venues vary
A "world's fair" of flower growing, with themed pavilions, reconstructed gardens and floral displays.

THE TULIPS

1 Above: *Tulipa* 'Jacqueline'

2 Left: *Tulipa* 'White Triumphator'
3 Below: *Tulipa* 'Mount Tacoma'

4 Overleaf Left: *Tulipa* 'Red Shine'
5 Overleaf Right: *Tulipa* 'Fringed Apeldoorn'

10 Below: *Tulipa* 'Mrs. John T. Scheepers'
11 Right: *Tulipa* 'Monte Carlo'

12 Overleaf Left: *Tulipa* 'Allegretto'
13 Overleaf Right: *Tulipa* 'Flaming Parrot'

14 Below: *Tulipa* 'Bellflower'
15 Right: *Tulipa* 'Fantasy'

16 Overleaf Left: *Tulipa* 'Black Swan'
17 Overleaf Right: *Tulipa* 'Blue Parrot'

18 Below: *Tulipa* 'Orange Favourite'
19 Right: *Tulipa* 'Salmon Parrot'

20 Overleaf Left: *Tulipa* 'Angelique'
21 Overleaf Right: *Tulipa* 'Menton'

22 Left: *Tulipa* 'Clara Butt'
23 Below: *Tulipa* 'Murillo'

24 Overleaf Left: *Tulipa* 'Candela'
25 Overleaf Right: *Tulipa* 'Georgette'

26 Left: *Tulipa* 'Bleu Aimable'
27 Below: *Tulipa* 'First Lady'

28 Overleaf Left: *Tulipa* 'Don Quichotte'
29 Overleaf Right: *Tulipa* 'Estella Rijnveld'

30 Below: *Tulipa* 'Fancy Frills'
31 Right: *Tulipa* 'New Design'

32 Overleaf Left: *Tulipa* 'Manon'
33 Overleaf Right: *Tulipa* 'Striped Bellona'

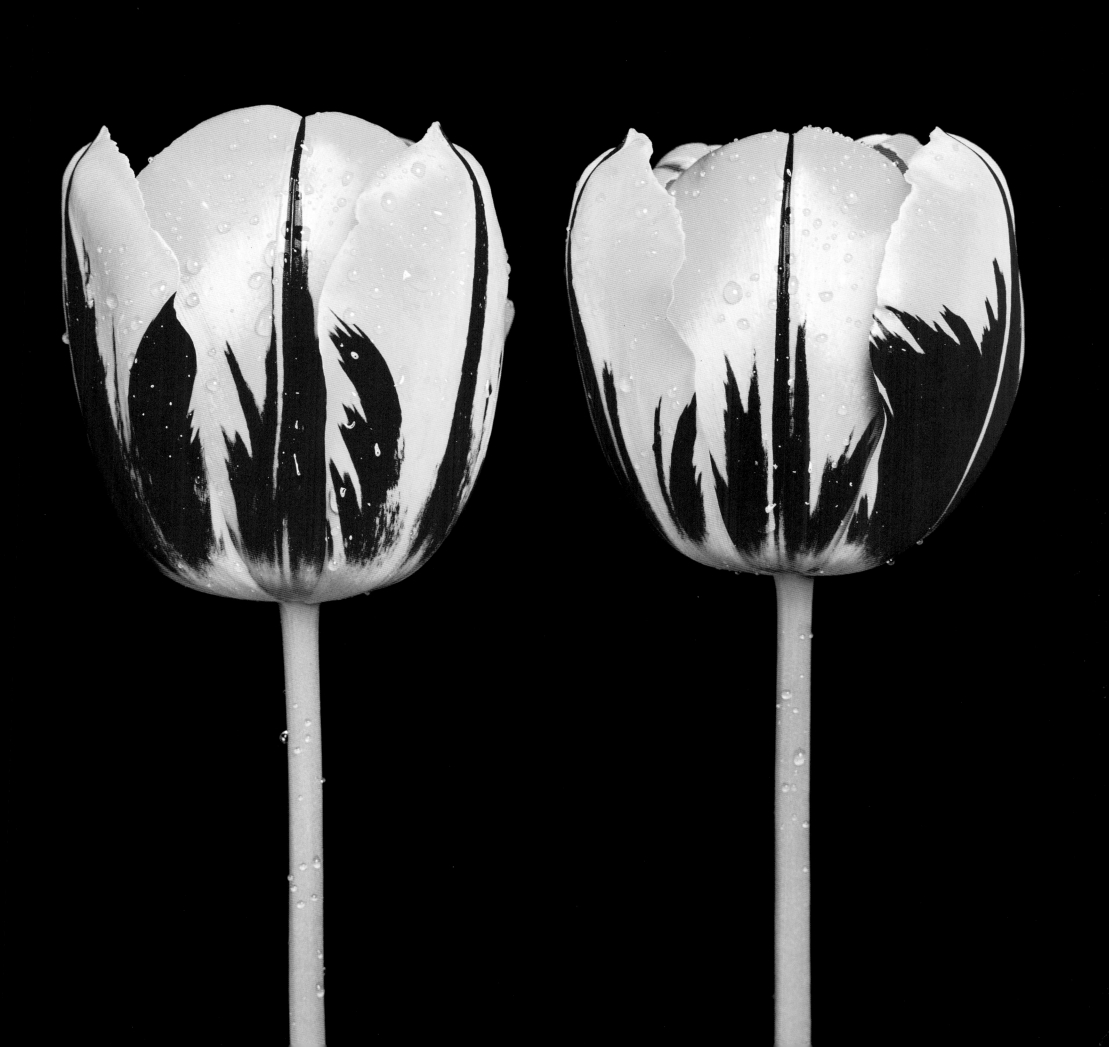

38 Left: *Tulipa* 'Latona'
39 Below: *Tulipa* 'White Parrot'

40 Overleaf Left: *Tulipa* 'Renown'
41 Overleaf Right: *Tulipa* 'Zomerschoon'

42 Below: *Tulipa* 'Maja'
43 Right: *Tulipa* 'Yellow Parrot'

44 Overleaf Left: *Tulipa* 'Garden Party'
45 Overleaf Right: *Tulipa* 'Lucky Strike'

58 Below: *Tulipa* 'Cordell Hull'
59 Right: *Tulipa* 'Twinkle'

60 Overleaf Left: *Tulipa* 'Habit De Noce'
61 Overleaf Right: *Tulipa* 'Black Parrot'

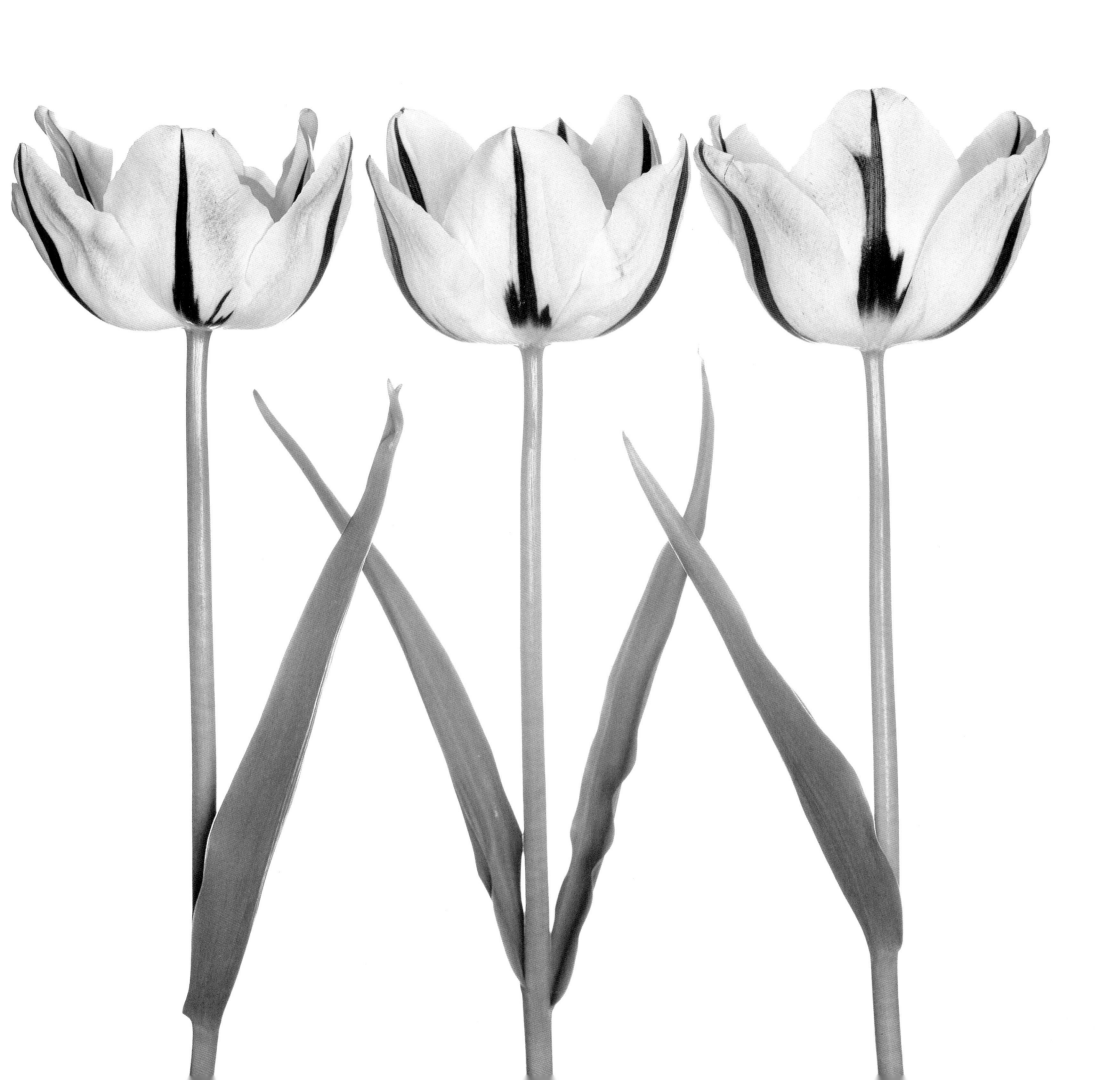

66 Left: *Tulipa* 'Golden Apeldoorn'
67 Below: *Tulipa* 'James Wild'

68 Overleaf Left: *Tulipa* 'Burgundy Lace'
69 Overleaf Right: *Tulipa* 'Christmas Dream'

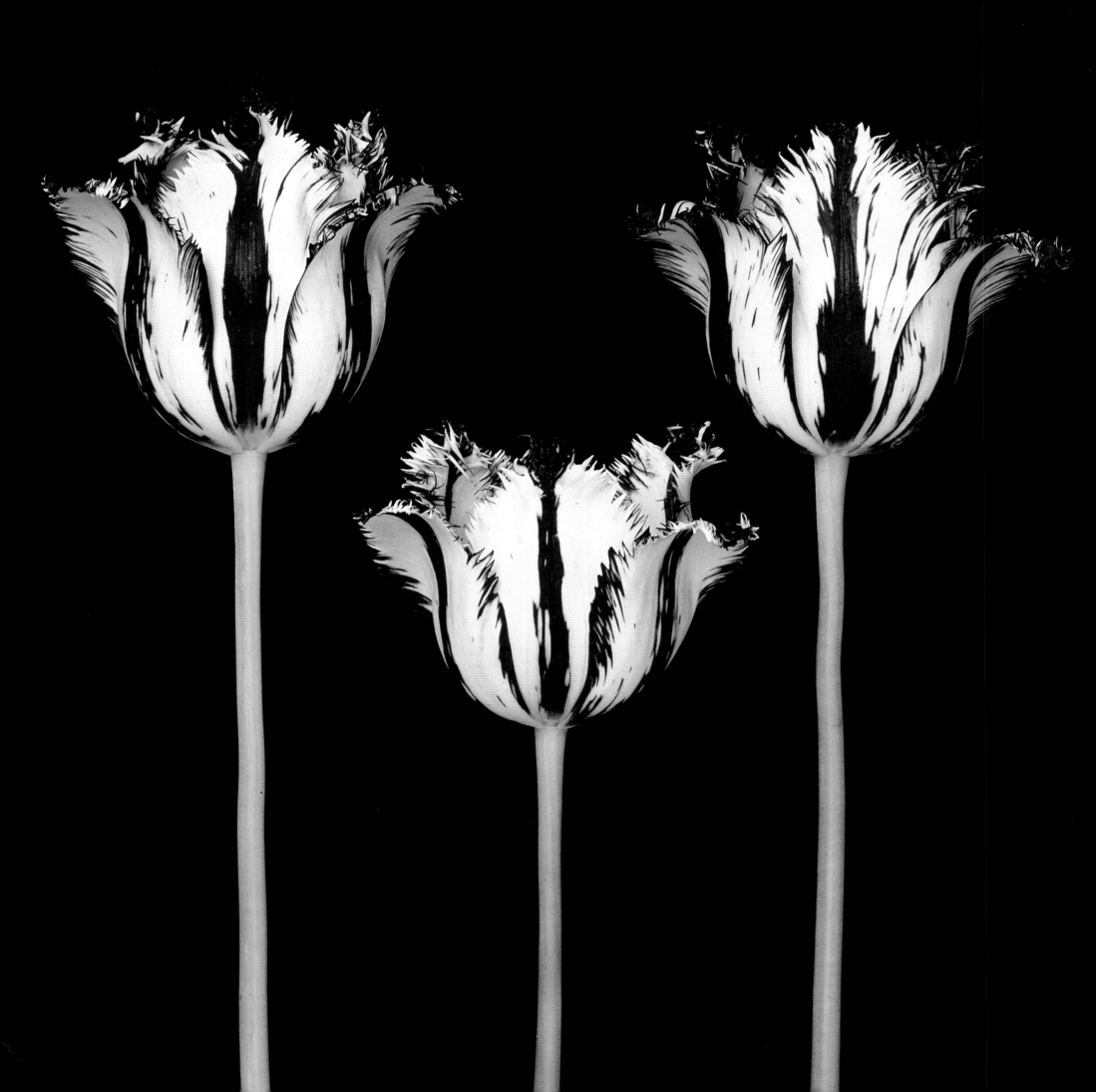

PICTORIAL INDEX

The figures shown refer to the plate numbers.

Tulipa 'Allegretto' (12)

Tulipa 'Angelique' (20)

Tulipa 'Attila' (52)

Tulipa 'Bellflower' (14)

Tulipa 'Bird of Paradise' (49)

Tulipa 'Black Parrot' (61)

Tulipa 'Black Swan' (16)

Tulipa 'Bleu Aimable' (26)

Tulipa 'Blue Parrot' (17)

Tulipa 'Burgundy Lace' (8)

Tulipa 'Burgundy Lace' (9)

Tulipa 'Burgundy Lace' (68)

Tulipa 'Candela' (24)

Tulipa 'Cashmir' (7)

Tulipa 'China Pink' (64)

Tulipa 'Christmas Dream' (69)

Tulipa 'Clara Butt' (22)

Tulipa 'Cordell Hull' (58, Back Cover)

Tulipa 'Don Quichotte' (28)

Tulipa 'Doorman's Elite' (48)

Tulipa 'Doorman's Favourite' (62)

Tulipa 'Elegant Lady' (55)

Tulipa 'Esperanto' (34)

Tulipa 'Estella Rijnveld' (29)

Tulipa 'Fancy Frills' (30)

Tulipa 'Fantasy' (15)

Tulipa 'First Lady' (27)

Tulipa 'Flair' (57)

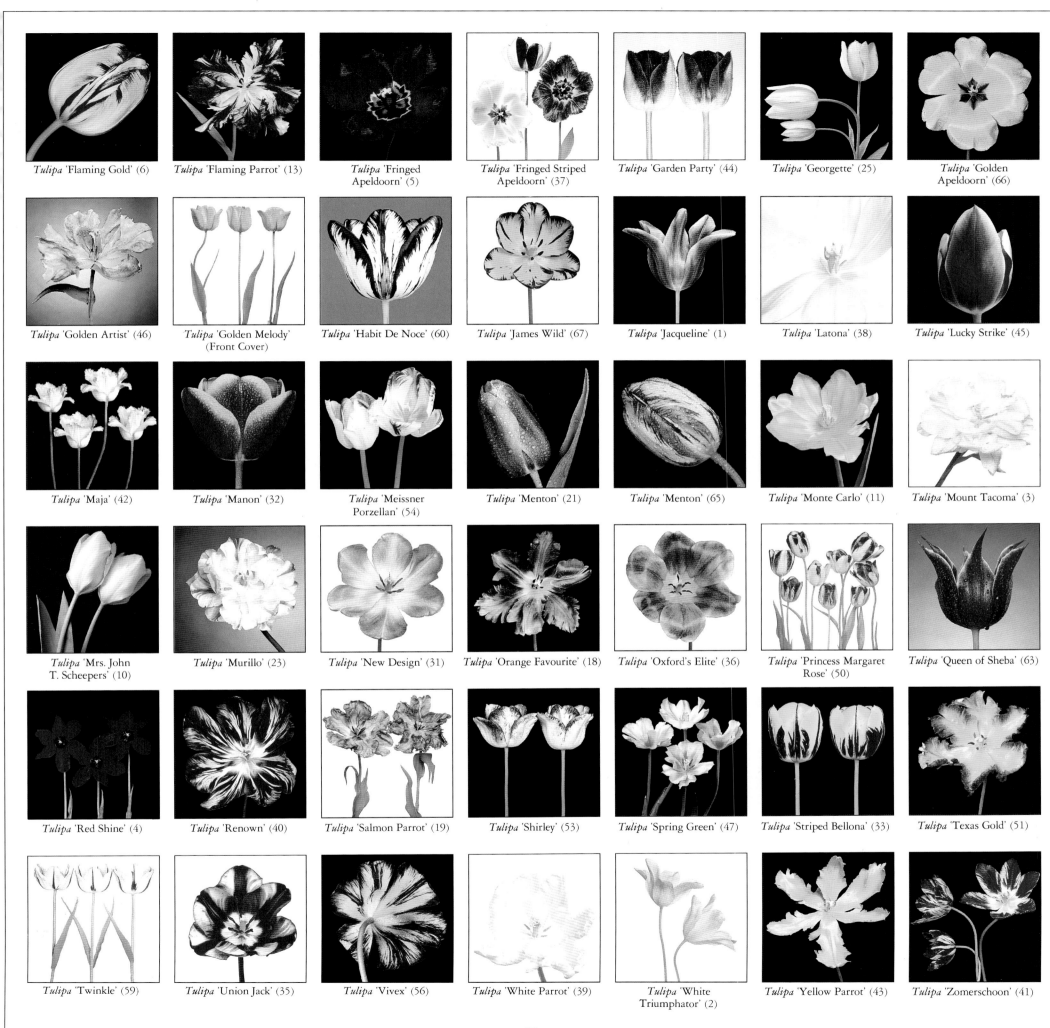

Tulipa 'Flaming Gold' (6)

Tulipa 'Flaming Parrot' (13)

Tulipa 'Fringed Apeldoorn' (5)

Tulipa 'Fringed Striped Apeldoorn' (37)

Tulipa 'Garden Party' (44)

Tulipa 'Georgette' (25)

Tulipa 'Golden Apeldoorn' (66)

Tulipa 'Golden Artist' (46)

Tulipa 'Golden Melody' (Front Cover)

Tulipa 'Habit De Noce' (60)

Tulipa 'James Wild' (67)

Tulipa 'Jacqueline' (1)

Tulipa 'Latona' (38)

Tulipa 'Lucky Strike' (45)

Tulipa 'Maja' (42)

Tulipa 'Manon' (32)

Tulipa 'Meissner Porzellan' (54)

Tulipa 'Menton' (21)

Tulipa 'Menton' (65)

Tulipa 'Monte Carlo' (11)

Tulipa 'Mount Tacoma' (3)

Tulipa 'Mrs. John T. Scheepers' (10)

Tulipa 'Murillo' (23)

Tulipa 'New Design' (31)

Tulipa 'Orange Favourite' (18)

Tulipa 'Oxford's Elite' (36)

Tulipa 'Princess Margaret Rose' (50)

Tulipa 'Queen of Sheba' (63)

Tulipa 'Red Shine' (4)

Tulipa 'Renown' (40)

Tulipa 'Salmon Parrot' (19)

Tulipa 'Shirley' (53)

Tulipa 'Spring Green' (47)

Tulipa 'Striped Bellona' (33)

Tulipa 'Texas Gold' (51)

Tulipa 'Twinkle' (59)

Tulipa 'Union Jack' (35)

Tulipa 'Vivex' (56)

Tulipa 'White Parrot' (39)

Tulipa 'White Triumphator' (2)

Tulipa 'Yellow Parrot' (43)

Tulipa 'Zomerschoon' (41)

THE CLASSIFICATION OF TULIPS

1. SINGLE EARLY TULIPS

"Single" implies that cultivars in this class have one flower head with six petals. Buds are slender and pointed, but in full sun the flowers may open out flatly.

Flowering time: Early to midspring
Height: 20–35 cm (8–14 inches)

2. DOUBLE EARLY TULIPS

The flower heads have double sets of petals, and flowers can reach 8–12 cm (3–5 inches) across when fully open. They have short, strong stems and the flowers are long-lasting.

Flowering time: Early to midspring
Height: 20–30 cm (8–12 inches)

3. TRIUMPH TULIPS

Mainly the result of hybridization between Single Early and late-flowering Darwin tulips, these flowers have an angular cup shape and there is a very wide range of colours. The group includes Mendel tulips — a result of crosses between 'Duc Van Thol', an early-flowering type, and Darwin tulips — which bloom slightly earlier than others in the Triumph group.

Flowering time: Midspring
Height: 25–40 cm (10–16 inches)

4. DARWIN HYBRID TULIPS

This class covers tulips resulting from hybridization between Darwin tulips and subsequent hybridizations between botanical tulips and other tulips. The flowers are perfectly shaped and can reach 17 cm (7 inches) across when fully opened. The colour range, though restricted to red, orange, yellow and pink, includes some of the most brilliant tulip colours: petals may show blotches or stripes.

Flowering time: Midspring
Height: 30–50 cm (12–20 inches)

5. SINGLE LATE TULIPS

This class includes late-flowering Darwins, breeder tulips and cottage tulips. These, with the Darwin hybrids, are the tallest tulip plants and the group provides some of the most popular bedding tulips.

Flowering time: Mid- to late spring
Height: 25–75 cm (10–30 inches)

6. LILY-FLOWERED TULIPS

These flowers are slightly waisted, with pointed petals turning outwards (reflexed). The blooms often reach 20 cm (8 inches) across when fully opened. Compared with other classes, there are relatively few varieties.

Flowering time: Midspring
Height: 35–75 cm (14–30 inches)

7. FRINGED TULIPS

This is a special class, all the cultivars having crystal-shaped fringes; many are mutants of the Single Late tulips. They are extremely popular although there are not many cultivars and the colour range is restricted.

Flowering time: Late spring
Height: 20–75 cm (8–30 inches)

8. VIRIDIFLORA TULIPS

The main characteristic of these flowers is their partly green petals, usually presented as a broad stripe from the base to the point. Mainly related to Single Late tulips, their shape is similar to that of lily-flowered blooms.

Flowering time: Late spring
Height: 30–60 cm (12–24 inches)

9. REMBRANDT TULIPS

These are the tulips that caused tulipmania in seventeenth-century Holland. The flowers have broken, variegated colours, usually striped: in other respects they resemble Darwin types. The broken colour is caused by a virus, so Rembrandts are not universally available: it is now illegal to grow them commercially in Holland.

Flowering time: Midspring
Height: 30–75 cm (12–30 inches)

10. PARROT TULIPS

These tulips are well-known for their unusual and exotic shapes, with fringed or feathered petals. The flowers are enormous, up to 25 cm (10 inches) across when fully open. The majority of cultivars originated as mutations of Single Late and Triumph tulips: forms depend upon the character of the parent plants.

Flowering time: Mid- to late spring
Height: 30–50 cm (12–20 inches)

11. DOUBLE LATE TULIPS

Also known as peony-flowered tulips, because of their resemblance to peonies, these large double flowers can be up to 20 cm (8 inches) across when fully open, and are borne on strong stems. Although there are few cultivars, there is a wide range of colours.

Flowering time: Late spring
Height: 30–40 cm (12–16 inches)

12. KAUFMANNIANA VARIETIES AND HYBRIDS

Also called botanical or wild species tulips, this class has been bred from *Tulipa kaufmanniana*, a species tulip native to Turkestan. The finely pointed petals open into a flat, star-shaped flower. They bloom very early, sometimes in late winter rather than early spring.

Flowering time: Very early spring
Height: 10–20 cm (4–8 inches)

13. FOSTERIANA VARIETIES AND HYBRIDS

This second category of botanical tulips derives from the parent species *Tulipa fosteriana*, native to the mountains of Central Asia. They bear large, blunt flowers, although the petals are pointed at the centre tip. All are vigorous growers and multiply freely. Some cultivars have mottled or striped foliage.

Flowering time: Early to midspring
Height: 20–50 cm (8–20 inches)

14. GREIGII VARIETIES AND HYBRIDS

These tulip strains, also classed as botanical tulips, are sometimes called peacock tulips, due to their bright colouration. *Tulipa greigii* is another native of Turkestan, and many hybrids have been produced from the species. An additional reason for their popularity is the leaf shape and markings, stripes or mottling in brown-purple, which create a decorative effect.

Flowering time: Early and midspring
Height: 20–30 cm (8–12 inches)

15. OTHER SPECIES AND THEIR VARIETIES AND HYBRIDS

This class covers over thirty botanical species and their varieties and hybrids. They are generally brightly coloured, but have smaller flower heads than the cultivars. Like most other species tulips, if left in the ground over winter, they will naturalize and form mature clumps and groups. They are not readily available in large quantities, but can be obtained through specialist growers.

Flowering time: Early and midspring
Height: 15–60 cm (6–24 inches)